Irresistible World Building for Unforgettable Stories:

A Creative Writing Guide For World Building That Sells

By Janeen Ippolito

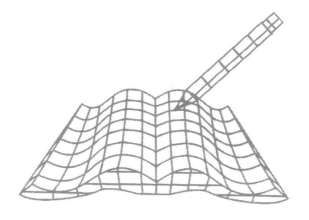

Copyright © 2018 by Janeen Ippolito

All rights reserved.

Cover design by Julia Busko
Editing by Sarah McConahy
eBook formatting by Sarah Delena White

No part of this book may be reproduced in any form or by any electronic or mechanical means including information storage and retrieval systems, without permission in writing from the author. The only exception is by a reviewer, who may quote short excerpts in a review.

Visit my website at **www.janeenippolito.com**

Table Of Contents

Introduction..5

Defining the Terms...9

Worldview..20

Characters...30

Narrative..42

Genre and Reader Expectations...53

The Final Element—Connecting with Readers....................................58

Dedication

To Sarah McConahy: where there's a "will," there's a way!

Introduction

In the realm of speculative fiction (science fiction, fantasy, paranormal, steampunk, etc.), fresh world building is one of *the* vital ways to attract readers. Fresh world building is cool. World building introduces new concepts and viewpoints that enthrall the mind and make readers spend extra time imagining and living in your story. That can lead to fan art, videos, cosplay, great reviews, and other celebrations of your work.

That being said? Creating ultra-fresh ideas can be a daunting task. A wise man once said there was nothing new under the sun, and he was right, especially in an age where novels are being released by the thousands *every day.* There are tons of stories about cyborgs, shifters, vampires, aliens, ghosts, space battles, and more retellings of fairy tales and myths than you can imagine.

The same internet you use to promote your world is there for every other author. Same ad services. Same social media platforms. Standing out in the crowd is more pivotal than ever to ensure your story is read.

So, what's the big secret?

Your goal is not to create an entirely new concept. Your goal is to focus on ways that *your* world building connects with *your* worldview, *your* characters, and *your* narrative in a style that makes your novel irresistibly unique. Well-integrated world building is like a well-made cake with just the right amount of filling and frosting.

Average world building will make people skim through your Kindle preview, but world building irresistibly fused with a unique worldview combined with compelling characters and narrative will push readers closer to the buy button.

Here are four questions to ask yourself:

1.) Worldview - How does your world building ask theme questions that reflect your view of the universe and resonate with readership?

2.) Characters - How does your world building create compelling characters who have to work through unique issues?

3.) Narrative - How does your world building push your plot forward with conflicts and problems that aren't found anywhere else?

4.) Genre/Market Expectations - How does your world building measure up to the expectations of your chosen speculative fiction genre and market?

Pretty hefty concepts—but have no fear! Throughout this book, I'll elaborate on each question and give practical action items to help improve your work. Read straight through or skip to the parts that interest you. Either way, you will come away with ideas to make your story shine brighter!

Notes:

Notes:

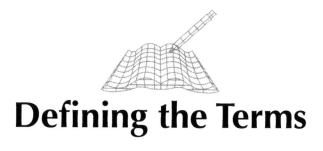

Defining the Terms

Worldview: The collection of personal beliefs, life experiences, personality traits, and physical characteristics that shape how a person views the world. Everyone has a worldview, and every author infuses their worldview into their story to some degree.

Even authors who are willing to write anything to make a buck reveal their worldview—that an individual's actions are disconnected from their beliefs, and what someone writes should have no bearing on their philosophies. However, the fact that many of the "write anything for a buck" authors use pen names for certain genres shows their awareness that readers (and possibly their family and coworkers) will form positive or negative opinions of them based on the stories they write.

Effective use of worldview to shape a story has a more potent impact than trying to hide from those effects. Because worldviews are based on deeply-held beliefs, tapping into shared beliefs can be a powerful way to reach readers. The Christian market in the United States uses this very angle. While known for Amish fiction and historical romance, the Christian market encompasses any genre that accepts, adheres to, and uses some version of Christianity as their foundational moral authority.

Using shared life experiences can also evoke reader sympathies. This is seen clearly in YA fiction, where many genres are bound together by the common themes and teenage life experiences of feeling awkward and left out, trying to discover one's identity apart from elders, and seeking to shape the world into something new. These universal coming-of-age themes play so powerfully that many adults read YA fiction as well. If an author can use their individual life experiences to offer a fresh perspective on these common themes, they can both satisfy genre conventions and the need for personal expression.

A key word in writing is *authenticity*. People want to know what you stand for. In sales, you want to know that a company will stand behind their products. In writing, you are a businessperson, and your book is your product. The more of yourself you put into your story, the easier it will be to sell it and connect with readers across social media platforms.

In terms of world building, worldview plays a key role in shaping the story, particularly the identity of races and cultures. Speculative fiction allows storytellers to shape the perspectives and core beliefs of their cultures in a way that no other genre of fiction can. Not only can authors use various races to make different arguments about different cultures, but they can insert their own worldviews and agendas into their stories.

Note: Because of the ability to insert worldviews, authors sometimes use speculative fiction as a way to aggressively push an agenda or belief. While this can be effective at reaching a certain audience, it can also alienate those with differing worldviews. The stronger the message, the narrower the audience. Whether or not you choose to force a particular issue is up to you but be advised that it will limit the marketability of your story.

There is nothing wrong with using your fiction to take a stand on something you are emotionally invested in, but choose your issue carefully and refine it so it comes across with fairness. Make sure you have a solid platform that clearly conveys the issue, and actively promote your agenda outside of your book so people with a similar worldview find your message.

Don't expect to suddenly convert people with opposing views. The best you can hope for is respect. Then again, the right level of controversy can attract attention, so who knows?

Bottom line: if you're using speculative fiction to promote agendas you are passionate about, and you are strongly convicted to make those messages clear and bold, then go for it. Just don't expect to suddenly make friends with people who disagree with those agendas. Your audience is people who agree with you and maybe people who are on the fence or who don't care. Whatever you choose to write, make sure your writing craft and storytelling ability are equally strong.

Theme: The theme of a story is the main idea. It's how the author's message is woven into the narrative. One way to discover the theme is by analyzing the character arc of the protagonist to see how they grow. This will indicate what the author thinks is good or bad. Another way to discover the theme is to examine the flaws of the villain(s). Sometimes the villain will be a clear concept: anger, hatred, selfishness, grief. Other times the villain will be a concrete person, place, or thing: a vicious mob boss, a horrible hurricane, or a devastating drug addiction.

Worldview and theme are inextricably woven together. Authors will always draw their themes from their worldview or modify a character's worldview to illustrate certain thematic conflicts or discussions. They can build their world in such a way that make specific themes inevitable. Or they can shape the plot in a way that brings up key questions or thoughts. The best book does all four to create a cohesive, enjoyable experience that avoids spelling out themes for readers.

Note: The more tightly woven the theme, the better a story will be. Trying to write a book without a theme is like trying to build a house without a frame; it's going to fall. Every story has one. From the fluffiest piece of chick-lit to the most action-driven suspense novel, every story has a basic theme embedded in it. Humans are natural meaning-makers and will find themes you might not even be aware of. The more you as an author know your theme, the more control you have over how you connect with your readership.

World building: World building is everything you make up as part of a speculative fiction story. Elves, dwarves, cities in the sky, hidden underground domains, new plant life, exotic foods—all of these are part of world building.

World building doesn't have to be all-encompassing, and it doesn't have to be an entire world. World building is simply anything you create in your environment that you have expanded and developed into a significant entity. In other words, it's everything you fabricated to attract readership.

Note: Excellent world building *always ties into or develops the plot or characters.* This is especially true of tightly-written contemporary fantasy, urban fantasy, and paranormal books where the story is driven by strong characters or plots. High fantasy, space opera, and hard science fiction call for a broad-scale approach, and readers of such will generally have more tolerance for sweeping stories and pages of description. Even then, you as the author should make that world building relevant to the plot and characters.

Now, you could argue that Tolkien wrote pages on hobbit culture at the start of *The Fellowship of the Ring* without solid relevance but remember that hobbits were key players in the overall plot of the book. Making them familiar and relatable only increases a reader's investment in the fates of Frodo, Sam, Merry, and Pippin. Through that introductory material, people are drawn into the Shire and made to see why that pastoral land is worth fighting for.

Even then, many people skip the description or skip the chapter "Concerning Hobbits" altogether. Because some readers find world building without context dead boring. Even if the author is Tolkien.

Characters: Characters make the story happen. They are the players, the agents, the reason the story exists. Their actions, their victories, and their defeats push the plot forward. They have to be intimately connected with the main conflict and the resolution.

Nail your characters, and you've nailed one essential building block of your story.

Characters will keep a reader interested when the story slows down. A solid character is no excuse for poor pacing or plotting, but a well-written, layered character with strengths and weaknesses will keep audiences reading. Moreover, if those character layers show off your world building or allow for additional narrative tension, then you will have created a compelling storytelling combination.

Note: Characters are necessary to your story, but *more characters aren't always better*. Building a solid cast of characters is like building a miniature golf course: each character should make sense to the whole, but each should be different from the others to justify their inclusion. Ultimately, the destiny of each character is to foil the protagonist, even though they might have secondary goals and arcs.

Narrative: Narrative is your story. The word "narrative" goes back to the word "narrator," the person in charge of telling the story. That person is you.

What story are you telling—and why?

Notice I use the word "narrative" instead of the word "plot." To plot is to plan and having a plan for writing is vital to the completion of your work. However, that plan is not the first thing you have to think about. You could have the best plan and the worst execution if the plan isn't letting you tell the story you want to tell. Good plotting is essential to good storytelling, but good storytelling is far more than just plotting.

Note: Narrative is one of the reasons stories succeed or fail. It's the element that pushes readers to keep turning pages, despite poorly-written characters, scant world building, and an army of grammatical errors. It's the essence of good and evil, of theme and purpose and message, that elevates all other aspects of a story.

I've plotted a number of books and learned a number of useful systems for doing so. However, I've abandoned or lost interest in projects because even though the story was solid, it had no *push*.

It didn't hit any of those crucial story-buttons for me. When you are crafting your story, hold tight to the things that fuel your passion. If you aren't moved by your words, how can you expect readers to be?

Application Questions

You can answer these yourself, but you can also repurpose them, asking them of others as they read your story. You might find that readers interpret your story differently than you do—and that could be a good thing or a bad thing, depending on your goals.

Worldview/Theme

What is the definition of good and evil in your story?

Who or what in your story holds moral authority?

What lesson does your protagonist learn? How do they grow?

What aspects of yourself, your beliefs, your journey, your personality, or your situation can you see in your story?

When others read your story, what thoughts or feelings do they come away with?

What elements resonate with your readership?

What is the message of your story?

What do readers think is the message of your story?

World Building

What are the key world building elements in your story? Is it set on a particular planet? Is a new race or species introduced?

If you have a lot of world building material, which parts are the most crucial to telling your story?

Which world building elements do your main characters interact with most often?

Which world building elements most strongly impact your plot?

Characters

Who is your main character?

What about that character makes them your main character? How do they uniquely interact with the plot in order to keep your story going?

How do your other characters act as foils to reveal different aspects of your main character?

What about your world building highlights that character's unique journey?

Narrative

What is it about this story that makes it urgent for you to take time away from other parts of your life and write?

If you had to tell this story out loud to people, what would be your reason for doing so?

What is the problem and solution in the story, and why does that matter to you?

What unique elements do you bring to the table for this story?

Notes:

Notes:

Worldview

Have you read the strategy on how to write a backlist of quick-read novels to get reader attention? What about the idea to drop the price of your first book to ninety-nine cents in order to snag readers and get them hooked on buying the rest of your series?

You've probably heard of these methods—and so have millions of authors all over the world. And while early adopters do well, and certain genres (romance and erotica) tend to support these with voracious readers, by and large these lead to market saturation.

Confession: I ignore most free and ninety-nine cent e-books these days. I may even forego the $1.99 and $2.99 e-books. Why? Because there are so many of them. It's content overload and taxes my limited reading time with too many options that I may or may not enjoy. And I'm not the only one.

What gets my attention in speculative fiction? Great world building executed smartly by an author who knows who they are, what story they're telling, and how to tell it effectively. An author who knows their motivations and their worldview.

Worldview—the set of beliefs, life experiences, values, personality quirks, and everything else that makes you a unique writer with something to offer that no one else on this planet has.

Own that authenticity. Know it. Use it.

Six Factors to Integrate Your Authentic Worldview and Motivation into Your Worldbuilding

Excite Your Passions

Do you love unicorns? Write unicorns. And do it your way, using your passions, creativity, and your unique perspective. What about vampires? Do you still like them, even though others say they're out-of-date? Or how about weird chemistry magic?

Whatever you can't get enough of, whether it be underground bunkers, dystopian societies, or faster-than-light travel, follow that passion. Don't be afraid of what is trending or of those who say, "That's been done before." Anyone who says that isn't part of your core audience. When you write from your passions, chances are good you will know the trends, the clichés, the stereotypes, and the must-have elements. You are your own expert, and there is no one better at writing your favorite subjects in fresh and satisfying ways.

Application
What is one aspect of your world building that you think is fun?

What is one aspect of your world building that you think your readers will like? Feel free to visit groups online or in-person where your readers hang out and see what excites them.

Challenge
What is one impossible bit of world building you've always wanted to stick into a story? Go ahead and write a short story or a piece of flash fiction with that world building, just for the fun of it!

Explain the Unexplained

What is something in your life you want to have explained? Have you had an experience you've never understood? Creating new worlds gives you the opportunity to answer questions in new ways. For example, what would it look like if the monsters under the bed were real? The answer to that question turned into the movie *Monsters, Inc.* What questions do you have that could be explored through your world building?

Application

Write down three situations, topics, mysterious objects, customs, etc. that you've never understood or always wanted to explain in a new way. Then write down speculative explanations for those things. Be as wild and crazy as you can!

Challenge

Choose a mundane object, custom, plant, weather pattern, etc. and write a short story about how it came to be. Ignore everything you know about this thing. Invent a new origin story or explanation that involves a different kind of magic or science.

Explore Your Feels

World building ideas come from your heart as well as your head. What situations or things break you? Chances are good they'll break your readers too, especially because you bring a personal passion to them. What do you enjoy? What makes you cry? What makes you angry? What excites you? Tap into these emotions and explore them in your story. An individual experience can be broadened into a universal theme, and that's something readers will relate to.

Application

Consider a situation that has had a profound impact on you, for good or ill. It could deal with loss (of money, of a person, of an object), love (of a person, of an object, of an ideal), traveling (away from somewhere, toward something new, etc.), or many other universal themes. Free write about that situation. Then imagine how you could transform that situation into a speculative story. How could world building uniquely shape that journey?

Challenge

Take a look at your current work-in-progress speculative fiction story. Identify key moments with feelings you identify with. Then broaden those themes to make the situation more potent—make it hurt more, exhilarate more, uplift more, or depress even greater.

Embrace the Quirky

Let's say you like popcorn. You really, really like popcorn, with all kinds of crazy toppings on it. You want to create a society where popcorn is a staple food? Do it. What about singing? Crazy colored hair? Or what if the major currency was buttons? World building is an excellent opportunity to embrace your quirks and elevate them to outrageous levels.

Application

Make a list of the quirkiest habits you or your friends have. How could you fit those habits into a speculative world? Note: if one habit is obviously taken from a friend, you might want to ask their permission first.

Do some research on uncommon animals, plants, geographical features, weather patterns, etc. Find at least five. Then figure out five ways you can push those features from the realm of ordinary to the extraordinary. (Warning: this may cause the sudden urge to travel.)

Research some real-world cultural trends. Don't just YouTube them or find one article. Do some in-depth research into the original meanings behind each cultural aspect. See if you can find individuals practicing those beliefs and ask them questions with an open mind. Then integrate an aspect of your research into your story world. Note: when doing this, work hard to be respectful of the culture you're researching.

Challenge

Create a flash fiction or short story built around three random aspects of your research. This is how truly creative stories can be made.

Engage Your Principles

Agenda fiction can be tricky to master, but if you want to pursue it, own it and do the best you can. World building is an excellent way to show the consequences of actions or violations of principle. Dystopian books frequently do this by having the main character stand up for freedom and justice against an oppressive or totalitarian society.

Application

World building in agenda fiction works best when you know your motivations and have a very clear sense of how you're using that in your world building. Some agendas have universal acclaim and can be obvious: human rights, anti-cruelty, treat others well. Other agendas, particularly those strongly tied to a particular religion or a divisive political opinion, can be trickier to manage. No matter how certain you are that your audience will agree with your message, continue to wrap it in solid world building. Find reasons in your story why this theme is an issue and embed it in the plot. And don't forget the shiny, quirky, feels-based world building!

Write down your hard message, then take a look at the other categories on this list and layer them over top each other in order to make the story work.

Challenge

Solid agenda world building is only as strong as its opposition. Take your agenda, make a thorough list of the opposing side's beliefs and arguments, then world build a story that successfully shows your agenda and the opposing side's.

Examine the Horrible

What could go wrong? This is a great question to ask in fiction because disasters are at the heart of stories. Consider the awful and how you could integrate it into your world building. All cultures and worlds have something wrong with them, so neglecting this part will short-change the narrative and realism in your story world. It might not always be fun, but going for the terrible and integrating it into your story is a great way to go.

Application

Consider the greatest elements of your world building and story, the unbreakable aspects of culture, religion, government, and geography. Write down a list of disasters and destruction and doom that could happen to each one or how each one could be twisted somehow. Go for the hurt.

If you're looking for extra ways to make things awful, consider your characters in reference to the world building. Write down a list of ways the world building could ruin their lives.

Challenge

Take a look at your work in progress. If at all possible, introduce more elements of doom and destruction, even in small ways. Heighten that tension and raise those stakes!

Encounter the Ideal

Utopian societies are challenging to create, partly because they lack narrative tension. If everything is going well, where's the conflict? Where's the story? Make things go wrong. Go ahead and indulge yourself in the ideals of a perfect society. Plumb the aspects of goodness, purity, and right, then destroy them in some way. You can do it literally (Alderaan was blown up in *Star Wars*, and the pearly planet Mul was destroyed in *Valerian and the City of a Thousand Planets*), or you could do it through motivation or origin (Amish woman falls in love with outsider—very common in Amish romances). In these situations, the tight, controlled environment has been threatened by an outside force. You could also threaten the protagonist with exclusion from utopia because of their issues. Make them feel the weight of knowing that they had the ideal and then it was snatched away from them. This is a great way to give a character a serious wound—and possibly turn them into a villain, if you're up for it.

Application

Create an ideal society. Start by thinking about all the problems in the present-day world, and then imagine a society where those problems would be fixed. What would it look like? Would it just be the culture that was ideal, or would it include the plants and the animals? What about perfect geography and climates? Write a list of potential ideals, then consider reasons why that society might be destroyed. Who would be against such a perfect place? How might the cost of utopianism affect the lowest of society? And what would happen if someone lost their place in that perfect world?

Challenge

Make something in your current story world ideal. Without blemish. Then write out scenes where your characters interact with this ideal. This exercise could reveal some new twists in your plot as well as some new aspects of your characters.

In your world building, feel free to sneak in the ideal. But remember to find that seedy underbelly, because no world is perfect.

World building that is synced with your motivations and worldview is world building that can't help but be unique. When you ask questions that stem from personal experience and inspiration, you create a one-of-a-kind narrative that will both fulfill genre conventions and reader expectations while offering your particular twist.

Creative, resonant world building comes from passion about a genre, personal fascinations, and your imagination. Allow your mind to twist and tweak your world building until it speaks to something that entirely thrills you.

Notes:

Notes:

Characters

Characters are the heart of your story. A good character will pull readers through an average plot, but an excellent plot won't forgive shallow characterization. Even characters who don't change over the course of a story need compelling elements that help them make sense in the overall narrative.

The key to creating great characters that interact with your world building is putting the character in situations with problems that can only happen in your setting.

Yes, good speculative fiction reflects life. But people also read speculative fiction to escape and explore a new world. In essence, if you're going to have cool scenarios, situations, concepts, inventions, land formations, or other such things, then make those aspects essential to the story. Have your characters interact with those world building elements (and maybe even *be* one of those elements!) in ways that could only happen in your specific context. Make it so that whenever readers consider your characters, they will associate them with your unique speculative location. Surround them with your creative magic, in large or small ways.

Ways to Integrate Your World Building into Your Characterization

Use the Character Issues
What is your character's main issue they have to overcome? Make it related to your world building. Maybe they have a lesser superpower. Maybe their space station was blown up. Maybe they failed an important test of educational ascension. Incorporate whatever problem they have into the world itself.

Application
Come up with a list of issues, either in your head or in freewriting. Note that protagonist issues come out of major changes in their lives. These changes are often disasters. If the changes are good things, then

these good things often clash with the protagonist's personality, goals, or natural abilities. In this "issue-driven brainstorming," come up with the issue *first*, then connect it with a character personality or character situation that will cause conflict.

Challenge

Take a look at your WIP, specifically the protagonist. What is their issue? How does it relate to the world building? See if there are ways you can enhance this connection so that the protagonist's journey can *only* take place in this story world.

Use the Character Arcs

Have a character's need to grow and change be predicated on something happening in the world you've created, and weave it into the storyline, for good or for ill.

Anakin Skywalker's negative character arc in the Star Wars universe is fed by the world building. Whether or not you like the Force being made of midi-chlorians, the fact remains that Anakin has a lot of them, and the Jedi Council (the quasi-religious and political entity that's a part of the world building) has to figure out what to do with this. Some believe he is destined to bring balance to the Force, but no one is sure what it means. Ultimately, some commentators think his tragic spiral into the Dark Side fulfills the need for balance. Since the Light Side won for so long, it's time for the Dark Side to have a turn! Whether or not you agree with this, the fact remains that Anakin Skywalker's tragedy is integral to the world building. His strength in the Force is directly tied to how his character arc progresses, and perhaps contributes to his fall.

In terms of a positive character arc, consider Tony Stark from *Iron Man*. Whether in the comics or the movies, he starts off as a part of Stark Industries, which counts as part of the world building in the alternate universe comic book world. Tony Stark inherited his company from his less-than-available father and has ambivalent feelings toward it, even as he uses the weapons technology shamelessly for profit. As Tony grows and changes throughout the story, so does his vision for Stark Industries—and his Iron Man suit and persona tie directly into both the world building and his desire for personal growth.

Application

What is your protagonist's character arc? Chart it out on a piece of paper by answering these key questions:

How does your protagonist think/feel/act at the start of the story? What is their issue?

How does your protagonist think/feel/act at the midpoint reversal or "mirror moment?" What's their moment of change?

How does your protagonist think/feel/act at the end of the story? How do they respond to their issue now?

How do the world building elements impact this arc? Are they part of the inciting incident? Are they involved in the character's midpoint reversal? What about the climax?

Challenge

Create a piece of flash fiction or short story where the character arc is intrinsically entwined with the world building. The world building has to involve one of the following elements:

Lunch food

Vehicle tires or wheels

Plants that spew a type of laughing gas

A major currency switch (for example, from paper money to cheese)

A talking park bench

Teleportation through some kind of visual display or television screen

An animal inheriting the throne of a kingdom

Note: If you want, feel free to share your short stories with me via my website, or email them to me at janeen[dot]ippolito[@]gmail[dot]com. I'd love to read what you come up with—and maybe even share it around my blog or social media!

Use the Character's Physical Issues

Give a character physical issues unique to your world building. In James Cameron's *Avatar*, the main character's condition as a paraplegic affects how he views himself and influences his choice to be part of a controversial colonization program. He's in it not just to help them, but to get the freedom of walking again. Connecting a physical condition, from an allergy to an illness or a special talent, to your unique world building, and using your world building to expand the condition, creates a winning story.

Application

What makes your protagonist physically unique or special? How is that brought out in the story? How can you use that element in the story more?

If there is nothing physically special or notable (includes brain giftings, emotional intelligence, etc.) about your protagonist, you should consider tweaking this. You are writing speculative fiction; this is the time to play! It doesn't have to be a superpower or unnatural ability. Ender Wiggin from *Ender's Game* had an awesome tactical brain that was a key part of the plot line. Consider how you could *challenge* or enhance your protagonist's role with some world building element special to them.

Challenge

Take one of your existing characters and give them a new physical *challenge* or issue related to the world building. I'm talking about losing a limb, gaining a powerful ability, losing a skill everyone else has, or some other serious, life-altering physical or mental change. Then make them live with it for the rest of the book. Don't give them an easy way out. How do they overcome this scenario?

Use the Character's Situations

Character situations should tie directly into world building elements. In the movie *What Happened to Monday?*, having more than one child is against the law, so the septuplet sisters hide in their apartment and pretend to be the same woman, each of them taking a different day of the week. Their names are even tied to their day. This creates a unique story situation within a dystopian universe. How can your character's situation connect with a world building element? Doing this enhances your story's potency, because now your character is intrinsically anchored in the world you've created, and your reader will be as well.

Application

Write out your character's situation and how it connects with your overall world building. If you're having difficulty making connections, consider the inciting incident of your story. This inciting incident disrupts your story's routine with a problem or change. At this key juncture, there should be world building connections.

Challenge

Create a flash fiction or short story based around a difficult world building scenario that profoundly changes a character's life. Go for the biggest, most drastic change or problem you possibly can.

Draft ideas here:

Use Cultural Interactions

Having a character interact with someone different from them (gender, age, socioeconomic status, race, etc.) is a valuable way to promote growth and change. When people are confronted with something new, it provokes a reaction of some kind. It can be complete acceptance, partial acceptance, amicable disagreement, angry opposition, or absolute denial. Any and all of these attitudes will force your character to deal with their issues.

Application

Here are some tricks to using interactions between different people. First, make their differences need to be distinct and notable. An age difference of one year won't be that significant, unless that's a critical year where your race undergoes a metamorphosis of some kind. Second, put the characters in a situation that makes at least one of them in a place of heightened emotional stress. This will ensure you have that all-important tension necessary for page-turning stories. Practice writing character scenes with these kinds of conflicts. Create unique ways of interpreting these conflicts through your world building. Here are a few ideas:

Gender difference

Age gap

Race difference (make sure both races are developed well)

Economic difference

Social status difference

Health difference (one is considered healthy, one isn't—or they are unhealthy in different ways)

Language barrier

Religious difference

Political affiliation difference

Personality clash

Physical endurance difference

Adaptation difference (they are built to withstand different climates)

Note: feel free to research cultural differences in the real world to get ideas. Just be careful how you use your research. Either research many different cultures and create a composite culture that doesn't strongly derive from one particular group, or research one culture, then find someone from that culture (who also reads your subgenre) to help you vet your story ideas and identify something is going to be offensive. Use charged areas with discretion. You'll never please all audiences, but make sure your perspectives will resonate with your particular audience.

Challenge

Go back to a WIP you have and identify any key differences between characters. Now enhance those differences and use them for moments of conflict. This conflict doesn't have to be drama. Humor often comes from light-hearted clashes over differences. It's all in how you handle it.

Use Prejudiced Interactions

Prejudice and stereotypes are universal issues because of in-group and out-group dynamics. Simply, this means we tend to prefer people we're familiar with in our inner circle and judge those outside that circle. In addition, stereotypes are a convenient way for us to put people into categories so we understand them. Stereotypes commonly originate from all of those cultural differences mentioned earlier.

Problems arise when we're forced to confront our presuppositions by interacting with others as complex individuals. Any kind of communication across racial, cultural, socioeconomic, religious, gender, ability, or other lines will involve conflict and character growth in some form. Or it may result in a refusal to grow, which is still a choice. Either way, incorporating these interactions in your world building through your characters can be a great way to add story tension.

Application

In order to write prejudice effectively, you have to dive into those sticky issues. First of all, figure out what the stereotypes are in your cultural world building. Decide where these stereotypes came from–misinformation? A legitimate cultural difference that is misinterpreted? Perhaps the result of a historical event, such as a war? Prejudice could even come from different physical preferences.

Whatever you choose, remember that these stereotypes can come from a cultural background or a personal background. An individual character can have prejudices based on their personal experiences that may have no connection with cultural stereotypes or prejudices. At the same time, an individual character can also reject cultural prejudices or stereotypes depending on their life experience, personality, or philosophy.

Also, be careful about drawing stereotype issues directly from real world cultures. It isn't forbidden, but it can be touchy. If you're going to go into touchy areas, do your research well, interview people, use smart beta readers, and be prepared to make someone unhappy.

Challenge
Add an element of prejudice to your story or enhance an element that already exists. This can be a small aspect or a large one. Doing a lot with prejudice and stereotypes can quickly get your story locked into agenda fiction (which isn't a bad thing—just make sure it is what you want). At the same time, ignoring prejudices ignores a great opportunity for conflict. If your culture exists with zero prejudices, how did that happen? Plumbing the depths of that "why" can be another great way to add world building.

Use Insurmountable Obstacles

Whatever is hindering a character's growth should be tied to your world building in some way. Growth arcs are universal, but how they are portrayed in speculative fiction can (and should!) be as diverse as the possibilities of your world building. Whether it's a dark lord or crazed supervillain, make the obstacle something potent, powerful, almost insurmountable—and something that could only exist in the world you've created.

Application

Try drafting a short story or piece of flash fiction with an insurmountable obstacle as the starting point. In other words, start with a problem, then build a world around solving that problem. This is a great method for creating short fiction on a specific theme for submission to magazines or an anthology.

Challenge

Analyze the obstacle in one of your WIPs. Make it more difficult for your protagonist by enhancing some part of your world building. This leveling up can mean physically increasing the difficulty of the obstacle, increasing the insecurity or issues of the protagonist, or making some aspect of the world building get in the way of the protagonist and the obstacle, such as how criminals often use legal loopholes to their benefit.

All stories have the power to reflect reality. Speculative fiction has the unique ability to do this and showcase spectacular worlds, impossible decisions, and incredible situations. The combination of reality and "what if" fantasy is what makes speculative fiction stand out among the various genres of literature. Make sure to embrace those aspects with characters whose strengths, flaws, *challenge*s, and joys are fully anchored in the world building you use to captivate readers on every page.

Notes:

Notes:

Narrative

There's one rule for integrating your world building and your narrative:

Write a story that can only exist within your world building parameters.

You've probably heard that speculative fiction is simply everyday fiction with dragons. On the surface that may be true, but dragons aren't a side note to the overall narrative. They are critical to exploring and conveying a unique story.

Good world building uses the creative elements of your imagination to drive the plot forward. It showcases a unique vision that can't be told with passion, purpose, or enjoyment in any other genre. It isn't mere window-dressing; it is integral to the plot. Otherwise, what's stopping readers from switching to contemporary fiction? Or historical fiction? Both of these genres give the same highs and lows to readers. Both genres have avid fans. Both can sell better, depending on your publishing strategy.

If you're going for speculative fiction world building, go all in.

Effectively using world building in your narrative will sharpen your story's appeal. Consider the following example I heard from author Mollie E. Reeder, who was writing a time travel story for a contest. She added a near-future setting to be cool, but since everyone in her story had advanced technology, the ability to travel through time wasn't seen as an irregularity. The author changed the setting to a contemporary one, featuring time travel as the key world building element. Honing her focus to that one unique element and weaving it into the plot made the story shine brightly.

Of course, now we come to the next question: how do you weave world building into the story without the dreaded info-dumping? Where do you put all that vital information?

First, make sure you know your genre. There are some speculative fiction subgenres where readers expect more information in large chunks. Epic fantasy is one of these genres. Urban fantasy is another, especially if the story is first-person POV and the information is relayed in a snarky, entertaining manner. Read a variety of books in your genre and study how authors integrate their world building in ways unique to that genre.

Second, use your plot points wisely. Below I've outlined key plot moments where world building needs to shine, as well as areas where you can insert world building elements into a plot and methods for doing so.

Embrace your weirdness, the unique parts of your story that reach your readers. Take your crazy ideas and make them work.

Key Areas to Focus on in Your World Building Narrative

Problem and Solution

When starting your narrative with a problem, make sure it involves key world building elements. If your plot could be dropped into another genre with only a few alterations, that's a warning sign. You can have corresponding themes and general situations, but your world building needs to affect the narrative in a remarkable way. If you're going to have a character get attacked by a dragon (as opposed to a dog) or sneak aboard an airship (instead of an airplane), figure out the details of those unique situations to add texture and layers to the plot.

World Building Inclusion

Write out the problem (what goes wrong or changes) and the solution (how the problem is solved) to your story. This problem and solution should be anchored in concrete details that are relevant to physical aspects of your narrative. Then check to make sure your world building elements are used effectively. If you can write out your problem and solution without any reference to world building whatsoever, then you need to tweak your plot.

Protagonist and Antagonist

Your protagonist and antagonist should occupy important places in your world building. However, they don't necessarily have to start that way. Katniss Everdeen is hardly a pivotal character in *The Hunger Games* when it begins, but her actions (as well as those of the Capitol, the main antagonist) force her into a place of prominence. Nothing in that story could properly exist without world building the dystopian government and the games. In the same way, your protagonist and antagonist should have distinct places in your world building that allows them to engage with your plot in compelling ways.

World Building Inclusion

One method that many speculative fiction writers (and fiction writers in general) use is making the protagonist enter a new world and become a key aspect of that world. This necessitates description of the world through the character's eyes as they encounter fresh obstacles and *challenge*s.

Another method is to create some kind of dysfunctional relationship between the protagonist and antagonist that includes world building aspects. This relationship can be law officer vs. criminal, government vs. rebel, family strife, mad scientist vs. escaped experiment, etc. Bonus points if you noticed that the examples in the previous sentence were power struggles. Power struggles are a universal source of conflict that can enhance your world building elements and story.

No matter how you do it, make sure your protagonist and antagonist interact with the world building in key ways that will give you a solid dynamic as you move forward through your story.

Introduction

Open your story with a scene that integrates your world building and setting in natural ways. Some speculative genres can handle opening with lots of information, but most stories benefit from a scene that displays the world building through character action and interaction with their surroundings. Allow readers to experience and discover the world as they join your characters on their adventures.

World Building Inclusion

Introducing world building from the start is vital, and it can be very tempting to info-dump. Depending on your genre, you might be able to throw in larger chunks of description. However, be wary of the "person walking down the street" method (which I will also dub the *Beauty and the Beast* opening song method). First, your character has likely been through that locale many times, so it wouldn't be natural for them to notice particular elements any more than you would notice your everyday surroundings when driving through a familiar part of town. While some characters might do this because they are bored, in many instances boredom only heightens a character's disinterest in their surroundings instead of intensifying it.

Instead, create a point of tension from the beginning of the story by introducing "a little unfamiliar" or "a little dissonance." This isn't the same as your inciting incident. You aren't disrupting your character's entire life. Rather, you're choosing to introduce a moment still within the confines of normal, but with a twist of the unusual. In Sarah Delena White's epic fantasy *Halayda*, the story opens with the main character, Sylvie, stressing over preparations for a critical event between the Fae and humans in her city. This event, a ball, occurs four times a year, and Sylvie has attended it many times as an assistant alchemist. The event itself isn't exceptional enough to be an inciting incident. However, the fact that it *only* occurs four times a year and is a tense situation critical to human-Fae relations makes Sylvie restless and nervous. Individuals who are restless and nervous tend to be more attuned to their environments or at least have a greater sense of them in particular ways.

This little bit of dissonance can take many forms, from a moment of bullying to a typical spy mission, or an evening walk with friends on an especially cold night. The key ingredient is to tip the scales a little to make the situation uncomfortable or different. Jar your characters just enough to give them a hyper-awareness of their setting. This will allow you to introduce your world's environment and characters in a natural way that allows readers to care about how the world building impacts the plot, instead of just admiring the window dressing.

Inciting Incident

Make sure your world building is featured in your inciting incident, aka, "the point where everything changes." If your story is based around time travel, then time travel should "change" in some way—either by a character traveling for the first time, or by something going wrong. If your world building elements revolve around a space station, have something threaten that space station. Use your world building to make that change-point stand out.

World Building Inclusion

Including world building in the inciting incident often involves creating ways that world building can go unexpectedly wrong. Space stations have sinister AIs. The One Ring needs to be returned to Mount Doom. The world building inclusion could also be something going unexpectedly *right*. In James Cameron's *Avatar*, a paraplegic gets the opportunity to be part of a revolutionary scientific exploration. When brainstorming new plots for stories, try to think about world building attributes that could go wrong—or right.

Midpoint Reversal/Mirror Moment

The midpoint reversal/mirror moment is the section of a plot and character arc when the protagonist goes from being the victim of their beginning issue to taking ownership of that issue and moving forward. In many cases it's an internal moment. However, what you can do is have that issue be related to world building elements so the character's confrontation with the issue can involve world building. If they don't fly spaceships because their father was killed on one, maybe the mirror moment is them choosing to walk voluntarily onto the spaceship for the first time.

World Building Inclusion

Carefully consider your midpoint reversal and see if there are small ways you can use world building to manifest the internal journey in tangible ways. It can be the character choosing to use a superpower they've previously forsaken or joining a futuristic organization they had a bad experience with. Any way that you externalize your character's inner journey will make your story stronger for readers.

Climax

The climax is the big moment in the story's plot. It centers around key decisions or choices that your protagonist will have to make. These choices are often a natural result of the character's arc in conjunction with the external plot. For example, in the book *The Hunger Games*, the climactic moment comes when Katniss Everdeen and Peeta Mellark threaten suicide by eating nightlock berries instead of continuing to play the game and try to kill each other. Whether she will admit it or not, Katniss has grown from a coal-town girl trying to save her sister into a rebel defying the system to protect her new friend and oppose injustice. Notice how this climactic action requires her to have internal growth (choosing to band together with others instead of working alone) and gives her an opportunity to reveal that internal growth in a way that integrates with the plot. Moreover, the world building elements of the Hunger Games and the made-up plant, nightlock, are pivotal to this climax. In the same way, your world building elements should be woven into your plot and character arc.

World Building Inclusion

Consider your inciting incident, your protagonist's issue, and their midpoint moment. How can you create a climax that will give the protagonist a defining choice to make? Are there world building elements you can create to enhance this moment? Climaxes are places where your world building elements can shine. How will you accomplish this? I recommend planning your climax in advance to ensure it makes your world building pop and delivers that intense moment readers want. If you write by the seat of your pants, then during revisions you will need to make sure your climax includes your world building.

Resolution

The resolution settles the problem of the inciting incident. If your resolution isn't doing that (at least in part), you need to fix it. The same goes for world building. Make sure your unique world building elements, woven together with the character arc, carry through the ending, and use those elements to solve the problem. One example of this is in the movie *Guardians of the Galaxy*. While the movie contains some fighting in its final moments, it also includes the entire team holding hands and working together to contain the power of the infinity stone—a key part to the story's overall world building. In this way, the movie shows Quill's character growth from a loner to a team player/leader and ties it into the world building elements. Excellent world building elements should weave into the plot and character arcs for a satisfying conclusion.

World Building Inclusion

How are your world building elements connected with your story's resolution? How are the problems your world building caused solved in a satisfying way? If you find that you don't have any key elements to resolve, that's a sign you need to go back to your inciting incident and use more world building to enhance your plot. Speculative fiction is built on world building. Make yours shine!

Note: If you're writing a trilogy or a series, you can leave some loose ends. However, you still need to know how those loose ends will work out in future stories. You will need to figure out your world building and your overarching plot lines in advance. This will save you a lot trouble later during drafting and revising.

Problem and Solution

World Building Inclusion

Write out the problem (what goes wrong or changes) and the solution (how the problem is solved) to your story. This problem and solution should be anchored in concrete details that are relevant to physical aspects of your narrative. Then check to make sure your world building elements are used effectively. If you can write out your problem and solution without any reference to world building whatsoever, then you need to tweak your plot.

Protagonist and Antagonist

World Building Inclusion

How do they interact? Make sure your protagonist and antagonist interact with the world building in key ways that will give you a solid dynamic as you move forward through your story.

Introduction

Open your story with a scene that integrates your world building and setting in natural ways. Some speculative genres can handle opening with lots of information, but most stories benefit from a scene that displays the world building through character action and interaction with their surroundings. Allow readers to experience and discover the world as they join your characters on their adventures.

World Building Inclusion

What world building elements are critical to the start of your story?

What is your Moment of Dissonance that will allow you opportunity to show those world building elements?

Inciting Incident

Make sure your world building is featured in your inciting incident, aka, "the point where everything changes."

World Building Inclusion

How is your world building featured in your inciting incident?

Midpoint Reversal/Mirror Moment

The midpoint reversal/mirror moment is the section of a plot and character arc when the protagonist goes from being the victim of their beginning issue to taking ownership of that issue and moving forward.

World Building Inclusion

Carefully consider your midpoint reversal and see if there are small ways you can use world building to manifest the internal journey in tangible, external ways.

Climax

The climax is the big moment in the story's plot. It centers around key decisions or choices that your protagonist will have to make. These choices are often a natural result of the character's arc in conjunction with the external plot.

World Building Inclusion

Consider your inciting incident, your protagonist's issue, and their midpoint moment. How can you create a climax that will give the protagonist a defining choice to make? Are there world building elements you can create to enhance this moment? Climaxes are places where your world building elements can shine. How will you accomplish this?

Resolution

The resolution settles the problem of the inciting incident. If your resolution isn't doing that (at least in part), you need to fix it.

World Building Inclusion

How are your world building elements connected with your story's resolution? How are the problems your world building caused solved in a satisfying way? If you find that you don't have any key elements to resolve, that's a sign you need to go back to your inciting incident and use more world building to enhance your plot. Speculative fiction is built on world building. Make yours shine!

Notes:

Notes:

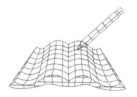

Genre and Reader Expectations

Genre and market expectations are a necessary anchor for your story. When your creative mind is exploding with fresh ideas, genre and market expectations provide you with a standard of how things have been done so you can figure out how to relate that to your book.

Some authors play it safe in this area and create their world building according to precise, well-known genre conventions. Alpha werewolves are always muscular and attractive. Vampires always get fried to a crisp in sunlight. The self-destruct buttons on spaceships always count down to zero before shutting off.

World building your story according to what readers expect is one way to make sure you reach your audience. After all, going off the beaten path with new ideas is risky. What if they don't connect with readers? What if your readers think it's weird to have your spaceships run on water or your dragons be vegetarians? These are fair questions. But they don't have to slow down your creative vision.

The middle ground is to take an existing genre and flip around some of the tropes and expectations while leaving others in place. In the television show *Farscape*, the ship is a living being—in other words, it's biological. This is a departure from the usual metal spaceships found in space opera and science fiction. However, the ship still conforms to audience expectations of a space ship, instead of a giant space worm. It still gets broken like a ship would and can be repaired with tools. In adhering to some expectations, the audience will be more likely to go along with the odder ones.

Here are some key questions to consider when thinking about how much to world build according to genre and reader expectations.

What are your goals with writing?

If you're trying to write and make money quickly, then writing to market and only tweaking small aspects of the expected world building could be good idea. Just be aware that you could be shoved into the category of derivative spec fiction and so lose readership. On the other hand, if you're writing to explore your own ideas, and you don't care about amassing a large readership, then go ahead with experimental world building. There is always an audience. It just might be smaller.

What do you know about your genre?

When testing your world building against the market, it is vital to know what your genre and reader expectations are. In order to know that, you need to have read a minimum of 3-5 popular books from that market. Can you write without this knowledge? Sure, but you'll be missing out on a lot of useful information about your ideal reader. Even if you're trying to experiment with something different, how will you know if you're doing that unless you know the standards? Reading in your genres is one of the best gifts you can give yourself as a writer and promoter of your stories.

Do your world building elements sound plausible?

Readers will accept even highly experimental world building a lot more readily if those elements are plausible. This doesn't mean they have to work in real life. It just means they have to make sense within the parameters of your story. Whatever rules you set up need to be obeyed within your story world and make sense to your target readership. If you're deviating from expected norms, those deviations also need to make sense.

What do your beta readers think?

Use beta readers who are fans of your genre. These readers can measure how close or far away you are from genre norms and whether or not it works for them. This feedback is invaluable.

Also, use at least 1-2 beta readers who are not fans of your genre. If they resonate with your world building, investigate why. Are you using tropes found in other, out-of-genre stories? Are you fixing something out-of-genre readers always disliked about that genre?

What if you find that non-genre readers love your story and genre readers don't? It will make marketing and promoting more challenging. The people who naturally like your world building elements won't like them (in this case), whereas the people who never usually like those world building elements will be hard-pressed to pick up your story because they won't recognize it as something they would normally enjoy. It will take careful branding and some reader education to connect with your audience. It's up to you whether or not you want to make that commitment.

Do you have enough expected elements?

Remember what I said before about *Farscape*? Apply it to your world building. By all means, make your spaceship alive, make your horses into carnivores with sharp, pointy teeth, or have your mermaids be terrible singers. Just keep other elements intact so your readers have something to anchor themselves in. In Charlaine Harris's Southern Vampire series, there is an artificial blood, called True Blood, that can meet the needs of vampires, making them less of a threat. However, vampires still have to sleep during the daytime, they still have fangs, and they're still immortal. Including some expected elements makes the unexpected ones easier to swallow.

Notes:

Notes:

The Final Element— Connecting with Readers

Investing in a speculative fiction story means thoroughly investigating the world building possibilities, creating wonderful elements with your author vision, and weaving them into the story in ways that make sense for your genre and audience.

Readers matter.

Readers who connect with your story world and get excited about it are some of the best and most natural marketing tools you can have.

Part of this includes investing in your story world, like including cool geography and cultural world building. Looking for insight on cultures? Check out my textbook and workbook, *World Building From the Inside Out*.

Another part is writing a story that is simply so irresistible that readers can't help but shout about it to whoever they can.

The final part is sharing compelling aspects of your world building online and in-person. Readers like cool things, and they like to share about cool things. Make that sharing easier by providing them with fascinating items, social media posts, or in-person moments. Social media strategies may change, but special items and memorable moments stand the test of time.

Here are some excellent ideas for sharing your story using your world building.

Create quote graphics that mention your world building elements. Mention that dragons are talking about scale mites or that the spaceship's engines are going to burn out. You can also use style and color elements that connect with your readership.

Share articles that inspired your world building. Make sure to connect particular elements in the article with your own story world. Also, make sure the articles are from reputable sources, especially if you're borrowing from another culture.

Dress up as your characters or the people from your story world—or find someone else who will! Even wearing a pair of earrings or a t-shirt can be a way to connect. People respond to visuals. Seeing visual aspects of your story gives them a tangible connection. Plus, it can connect you to superfans.

Create art or book swag that connects with your story. If you're a creative type, use your art as a way to connect with your audience and your overall story brand. At conventions, I noticed how people would come up to my table for the steampunk decorations and then want to buy them. I realized if I had decorations I could sell, then I could provide something people wanted and also have something to use in giveaways. Plus, people love sharing pictures of those objects online, and I get a break from my computer screen. Winning situation!

Note: You need to have a certain level of skill in your art to make this work. However, for a small fee, either to a graphic designer or for some self-tutorials on graphic design, you can create and order bookmarks, buttons, and other book swag for less time. Just putting your book cover on a bookmark can be enough—and of course, your book cover includes some suggestion of your world building elements anyway, right?

Get inspiration from your friends for your world building. I have a friend who is an entomologist (insect expert) and also has knowledge of plants. She's been the main inspiration for one of my cultures, a plant-type of people who interact with insects on a daily basis. We've worked together at a science camp for several summers, and I've been able to use the fascinating elements I've learned in my world building. As a bonus, I can say that my world building was vetted by an expert who is curious about and invested in my work!

Ultimately, world building that sells comes down to your vision, your goals, your market, and your writing craft.

Whenever possible, connect your world building with your worldview, your characters, and your narrative. Weave it so tightly into your plot that the only way you can tell the story in a potent way is by using the world building elements. Doing so will make your story unique, vibrant, and more marketably you.

And that is always a good thing.

Acknowledgements

First, I am and always will be forever grateful to my Creator for making me and making our amazing world.

Major thanks to Stephen Ippolito Jr, my husband, fellow geek, and educator extraordinaire. Brainstorming questions and ideas with you is the best thing ever!

Additional gratitude to beta readers Tina Yeager, Heather Polczynski, Mollie Reeder, and Hannah Williams. Thank you for taking your time and giving great feedback.

My appreciation goes out to Sarah McConahy for the line editing and copy editing. Working with you is always an adventure in meaning, grammar details, and which rules to break. I wouldn't have it any other way!

Also, thanks to Sarah Delena White for the e-book formatting and for pushing me to keep at this book no matter what.

And thanks to Julia Busko for the cover design, especially for your patience with finding just the right shade of green.

About the Author

Janeen Ippolito believes words transform worlds. She writes urban fantasy and steampunk, and creates writing resources, including the reference book *World Building From the Inside Out* and the creative writing guide *Irresistible World Building For Unforgettable Stories*. She's an experienced teacher, editor, author coach, and is the leader of Uncommon Universes Press, a small science fiction and fantasy publishing house. She's also the cohost of the podcast Indie Book Magic. In her spare time, Janeen enjoys sword-fighting, reading, pyrography, and eating brownie batter. Two of her goals are eating fried tarantulas and traveling to Antarctica. This extroverted writer loves getting connected, so find her on Twitter, Facebook, Instagram, and at her website: janeenippolito.com

Additional Help

Thanks for reading!

Please leave a review online (Amazon.com, Barnes and Noble, Goodreads) giving feedback and mentioning any ways this book helped you. I love feedback! Feedback leads to more books.

For additional help, check out my website and sign up for my newsletter!
www.janeenippolito.com

Also, feel free to connect with me online with any further questions, or just to say hello!

Facebook: www.facebook.com/janeenippolito
Pinterest: www.pinterest.com/janeen_ippolito
Twitter: twitter.com/JaneenIppolito
Instagram: instagram.com/janeen_ippolito

Made in the USA
Lexington, KY
19 December 2018